REFLECTIONS
FOR **DAILY PRAYER**

REFLECTIONS
FOR **DAILY PRAYER**
ADVENT TO **EPIPHANY**
3 DEC 2007 – 2 FEB 2008

GORDON MURSELL
STEPHEN COTTRELL
PAULA GOODER
JANE WILLIAMS

CHURCH HOUSE
PUBLISHING

Church House Publishing
Church House
Great Smith Street
London SW1P 3AZ

Tel: 020 7898 1451
Fax: 020 7898 1449

ISBN 978 0 7151 4145 8

Published 2007 by Church House Publishing
Copyright © The Archbishops' Council 2007

The opinions expressed in this book are those of the
authors and do not necessarily reflect the official
policy of the General Synod or The Archbishops'
Council of the Church of England.

Designed by Hugh Hillyard-Parker

Printed by Creative Print and Design Group Ltd,
Blaina, Wales

Contents

About the authors

Gordon Mursell is the Bishop of Stafford. He is in constant demand as a speaker and teacher of the faith. He has written the two-volume *English Spirituality* and taught widely from the Scriptures.

Stephen Cottrell is the Bishop of Reading. He is a popular speaker, evangelist, author of *Do Nothing to Change Your Life* and co-author of the *Emmaus: The Way of Faith* series.

Paula Gooder teaches New Testament at the Queen's Foundation in Birmingham and also works freelance as a writer and lecturer in Biblical Studies. She is a Reader in the Church of England and a member of the General Synod.

Jane Williams is a popular writer. She lectures at St Paul's Theological Centre and is a visiting lecturer at King's College London. She taught previously at Trinity Theological College, Bristol.

About *Reflections for Daily Prayer*

Based on the *Common Worship Lectionary* readings for Morning Prayer, these daily reflections are designed to refresh and inspire times of personal prayer. The aim is to provide rich, contemporary and engaging insights into Scripture.

Each page lists the lectionary readings for the day with the main psalms for that day highlighted in bold. The Collect of the day – either the *Common Worship* collect or the shorter additional collect – is also included.

A short reflection is provided on either the Old or New Testament reading. Popular writers, experienced ministers, biblical scholars and theologians will be contributing to this series. They all bring their own emphases, enthusiasms and approaches to biblical interpretation to bear.

Regular users of Morning Prayer and *Time to Pray* (from *Common Worship: Daily Prayer*) and anyone who follows the lectionary for their regular Bible reading will benefit from the rich variety of traditions represented in these stimulating and accessible pieces.

Monday 3 December

Isaiah 25.1-9

It is not clear what city is being referred to here, but it symbolizes human greed and ruthlessness. As with the Tower of Babel, God has reduced it to ruins and revealed himself instead as a refuge to the poor (25.4). So the God of Advent is a God who will overturn worldly structures of power and raise up the lowly. And what is really striking, in the midst of all this upheaval, is the wonderfully attractive vision of a new future we find in verses 6-9. In the Bible, such visions are always born out of exile or some kind of disorder: it's just when you might expect the people of God to be giving up hope, or turning in on themselves, that God seems to grant them amazing new visions of a renewed cosmos. A Church that is strong and secure has little interest in nurturing such visions, but a Church that is facing an uncertain future can be precisely the seedbed for a new and compelling vision of how the world could be.

Advent is the ideal season to ask yourself: what kind of vision do I have, and how can I help my local church to develop a vision, rooted in texts such as this, that will bring hope not just to the church itself but to all creation?

COLLECT

Almighty God,
give us grace to cast away the works of darkness
and to put on the armour of light,
now in the time of this mortal life,
in which your Son Jesus Christ came to us in great humility;
that on the last day,
when he shall come again in his glorious majesty
   to judge the living and the dead,
we may rise to the life immortal;
through him who is alive and reigns with you,
in the unity of the Holy Spirit,
one God, now and for ever.

Psalms **80**, 82 *or* **5**, 6, 8
Isaiah 26.1-13
Matthew 12.22-37

Isaiah 26.1-13

It is hard for those of us lucky enough to live in a free and relatively prosperous society to imagine how life must be for those who do not enjoy these things. This passage comes alive if we read it as the vision (verses 1-6) and the prayer (verses 7-13) of those who live in one of the world's most impoverished and violent societies. Notice the language of desire and longing (verse 9), and the passionate visualizing of a new and different world order (verses 1 and 12). Part of the Church's task during the season of Advent is to lift up in prayer those who might offer these words today, and especially those who may feel they have no future.

The God of Advent is above all else a God who brings a new future to those who feel trapped in despair and hopelessness – victims of urban violence or rural poverty – but also to those who can see no sign of a better life either for them or for their children. Again and again in Scripture, God brings new life and hope into the midst of situations like these – and perhaps our persistent and prophetic prayer can help God do the same again today.

Almighty God,
as your kingdom dawns,
turn us from the darkness of sin to the
light of holiness,
that we may be ready to meet you
in our Lord and Saviour, Jesus Christ.

COLLECT

3

Wednesday 5 December

Psalms 5, **7** *or* **119.1-32**
Isaiah 28.1-13
Matthew 12.38-end

Isaiah 28.1-13

In this ferocious passage, God calls into question the future of those who take that future for granted. As our world faces the looming threats of climate change and global warming, it is worth noting how the prophet uses the imagery of extreme climatic events ('like a storm of hail, a destroying tempest, like a storm of mighty, overflowing waters', 28.2) to describe how God will bring catastrophe on a society mired in greed and over-indulgence.

It is not God's fault: it is the inevitable consequence of failing to pay attention to God's word ('Therefore the word of the Lord will be to them, "Precept upon precept"', 28.13) and of putting our own short-term convenience before the long-term interests of our cosmos.

Even here, though, there is hope ('In that day the Lord of hosts will be a garland of glory ... to the remnant of his people', 28.5). But the Advent hope is salted with judgement and fire: only a radical reorientation of our priorities will allow us to recover the future that is now critically under threat. This is nothing less than an urgent wake-up call for the planet.

COLLECT

Almighty God,
give us grace to cast away the works of darkness
and to put on the armour of light,
now in the time of this mortal life,
in which your Son Jesus Christ came to us in great humility;
that on the last day,
when he shall come again in his glorious majesty
   to judge the living and the dead,
we may rise to the life immortal;
through him who is alive and reigns with you,
in the unity of the Holy Spirit,
one God, now and for ever.

Psalms **42**, 43 *or* 14, **15**, 16
Isaiah 28.14-end
Matthew 13.1-23

Isaiah 28.14-end

The message of these verses is clear: only faith in God can save us from the 'overwhelming scourge' that is to come (28.18). It isn't clear what that scourge will be: it could represent any one of a range of natural or human-induced disasters. What is clear is that, even under the threat of either physical or moral tsunami, God is already laying the foundations for a new world order, based on 'a precious cornerstone' (28.16), which for Christians is Jesus Christ.

The crucial thing is not to 'scoff' (28.22) – in other words, to laugh at the threat of catastrophe. Advent is above all else a time for sober reflection on the future of ourselves and our planet, and these great prophecies of Isaiah provide the ideal resources for doing this. What matters is to 'listen, and ... pay attention' (28.23), for the Lord is 'wonderful in counsel, and excellent in wisdom' (28.29). Wisdom is not the same as cleverness, although we often confuse the two: cleverness may get you a job, but it won't help you face the future with faith and hope. Only wisdom, the fruit of a life lived in trusting dependence on God, can equip us to do that.

Almighty God,
as your kingdom dawns,
turn us from the darkness of sin to the
light of holiness,
that we may be ready to meet you
in our Lord and Saviour, Jesus Christ.

COLLECT

Isaiah 29.1-14

In these verses, the prophet warns of a coming attack on Jerusalem (also referred to as Ariel here). The attack will be terrifying, but not ultimately successful, because God will protect the city from the invaders. The crucial question is: will the inhabitants of the city learn from this experience, or will they take refuge in introspective slumber (see 29.10)?

The text may well refer to the ferocious onslaught against Jerusalem by the Assyrians under Sennacherib, but it holds a wider meaning for us. How do we respond to events that shake our faith to the core – the sudden discovery of a malignant tumour, or the loss of a loved one, or a violent and unprovoked attack on an innocent person or group? Advent offers us a unique and precious opportunity to open our eyes to the reality of the world around us, in all its mixture of beauty and evil – and not to take refuge in illusion. But we are also invited to open our eyes to see God at work within and around us, a God who is never safe or domesticated or narrowly churchy, and a God who deserves not empty worship (see 29.13), but heartfelt devotion and childlike trust.

COLLECT

Almighty God,
give us grace to cast away the works of darkness
and to put on the armour of light,
now in the time of this mortal life,
in which your Son Jesus Christ came to us in great humility;
that on the last day,
when he shall come again in his glorious majesty
to judge the living and the dead,
we may rise to the life immortal;
through him who is alive and reigns with you,
in the unity of the Holy Spirit,
one God, now and for ever.

Isaiah 29.15-end

It is temptingly easy to regard God as our own invention. People of faith would never admit such a thing, but in practice it is perfectly possible to behave as though God doesn't exist, or as though God is simply the sum of all the things we happen to approve of. Many horrendous crimes have been committed in the name of a self-serving religion, which seeks to reduce God to a mascot or national flag, entirely powerless to challenge us. But Isaiah says that to do that is to regard the potter as the clay (29.16), when the reality is the other way round.

The great danger we face is to let religion take the place of God. But the true God is above religion, and not restricted to any one manifestation of it. This God is constantly working to subvert duplicity and arrogance (29.15,20), and to raise up the meek and the neediest people (29.19). And the surest sign of such a God is a sign Jesus himself will later emphasize: a child (see 29.23). Only those who are willing to replace their own prejudices with true childlike trust in God will inherit the kingdom God has in mind for us.

Almighty God,
as your kingdom dawns,
turn us from the darkness of sin to the
light of holiness,
that we may be ready to meet you
in our Lord and Saviour, Jesus Christ.

COLLECT

Monday 10 December

Psalms **44** *or* 27, **30**
Isaiah 30.1-18
Matthew 14.1-12

Isaiah 30.1-18

The message of these verses is both relevant and challenging in our day: do not assume that politically expedient alliances will be any substitute for a genuine willingness to listen to what God is saying. The prophet criticizes children who will not hear the instruction of the Lord (30.9), and warns them against assuming that rushing into an alliance with Egypt will help them. Indeed, this passage is a sustained critique, not just of political machinations but of frenzied activism of any kind. For both have the effect of putting ourselves in the place of God.

The beautiful conclusion to this passage points to the true moral, and the true message of Advent: we need to learn to wait, not with the apathetic indifference of those who have nothing to look forward to, but with the active, expectant alertness of those who know God's kingdom is coming. Rich and powerful people are bad at waiting for anything, and find it hard when they have no choice but to wait – for news about their health, for example – whereas the poor know what it is to wait in hope: 'Therefore the Lord waits to be gracious to you ... For the Lord is a God of justice; blessed are all those who wait for him' (30.18).

COLLECT

O Lord, raise up, we pray, your power
and come among us,
and with great might succour us;
that whereas, through our sins and wickedness
we are grievously hindered
in running the race that is set before us,
your bountiful grace and mercy
may speedily help and deliver us;
through Jesus Christ your Son our Lord,
to whom with you and the Holy Spirit,
be honour and glory, now and for ever.

Tuesday 11 December

Isaiah 30.19-end

In this passage, we are shown the positive consequences of a willingness really to listen to God. Even in times of affliction, 'your eyes shall see your Teacher. And when you turn to the right or when you turn to the left, your ears shall hear a word behind you, saying, "This is the way; walk in it"' (30.20-21).

More important still, a society willing to pay attention to God's word and guidance will become a blessing for the whole earth: it is very important to see how in this passage the well-being of the earth is linked to the well-being of the people of God. A community that waits on God will witness the gift of rain: 'on every lofty mountain and every high hill there will be brooks running with water' (30.25). In a world in which millions of humans and creatures suffer from drought that is almost certainly linked to global warming, this text has urgent contemporary relevance. And it concludes with a new linkage – between the defeat of enemies and oppressors and the making of music (30.29-31). Advent is the season for looking forward in hope, and we are offered here a compelling and attractive vision of the new world order God longs to bring to birth – and of how we can play our part in advancing it.

Almighty God,
purify our hearts and minds,
that when your Son Jesus Christ comes again as
judge and saviour
we may be ready to receive him,
who is our Lord and our God.

COLLECT

Wednesday 12 December

Psalms **62**, 63 *or* **34**
Isaiah 31
Matthew 15.1-20

Isaiah 31

What image of God do you prefer? For some, the image of an old man with a beard reigning from a heavenly throne is hard to shake off, even though the Bible makes it clear that God is above and beyond all images. Even so, this passage offers us two, both of them drawn from the natural world. The first is the lion (31.4), an image of fearless courage and steadfastness. The second, more surprisingly (although it is found in the Psalms as well), is that of birds hovering overhead (31.5). This is an image of protection and shelter. We may not see God, but God is for us like a mother bird hovering high above its young, watchfully protecting them from predators and danger.

Belief in God does not insure us against bad things happening to us, but it does ensure, first that we no longer have to face these things on our own, and secondly that nothing can finally separate us from the reach of God's loving care. As we reflect on and pray about our own future and that of our cosmos during the season of Advent, the promise of God's enduring love encourages us to face that future with realism but also with hope.

COLLECT

O Lord, raise up, we pray, your power
and come among us,
and with great might succour us;
that whereas, through our sins and wickedness
we are grievously hindered
in running the race that is set before us,
your bountiful grace and mercy
may speedily help and deliver us;
through Jesus Christ your Son our Lord,
to whom with you and the Holy Spirit,
be honour and glory, now and for ever.

Psalms 53, **54**, 60 *or* 37
Isaiah 32
Matthew 15.21-28

Isaiah 32

In this tremendous chapter we are offered a powerful vision of a renewed cosmos, coupled with an urgent warning not to be complacent (32.9-10), or to take the *status quo* for granted. The prophet warns of hard times ahead, in which palaces and cities that had been joyous and jubilant (32.13) will, in a striking reversal, become 'the joy of wild asses, a pasture for flocks' (32.14).

In these hard times, the fortunes of human beings and of the animal creation are sharply opposed to one another. But the prophet sees this as the still-avoidable consequence of human complacency and short-term thinking; for beyond that, if we can trust in God, we can look forward to a time when justice will dwell in the wilderness, and when both human beings and animals can inhabit the earth in peace and freedom.

This is the vision we forfeited in Eden, yet this is also the vision, renewed and enlarged, that God summons us to assist in bringing to birth. Nothing less than this is good news for our world.

Almighty God,
purify our hearts and minds,
that when your Son Jesus Christ comes again as
judge and saviour
we may be ready to receive him,
who is our Lord and our God.

COLLECT

11

Friday 14 December

Isaiah 33.1-22

After an opening denunciation of evil power, the prophet offers us a marvellous Advent prayer: 'O Lord, be gracious to us; we wait for you. Be our arm every morning, our salvation in the time of trouble' (33.2). But the following song of praise swiftly gives way to the language of lament (33.7) as the people pour out to God their present experience of lawless chaos and disorder (33.8-9). You will be able to think of people in the world who might pray these verses today, and offer them as a prayer for them yourself.

And the prayer of lament, as so often in Scripture, triggers a response from God (33.10): the spirituality of Advent needs to be honest, world-embracing, not narrowly introspective or pious, if we are to engage as we should with the great threats to our world and thus allow ourselves to become partners with God in renewing the creation. And notice here, yet again, how the future of humanity and the future of the cosmos are inextricably linked: the imagery throughout these verses is drawn from the natural world. Those who live righteously will also live in partnership with the natural order around them; and the Lord in majesty is described as 'a place of broad rivers and streams' (33.21), an image of inexhaustible fruitfulness for humans and creatures alike.

COLLECT

O Lord, raise up, we pray, your power
and come among us,
and with great might succour us;
that whereas, through our sins and wickedness
we are grievously hindered
in running the race that is set before us,
your bountiful grace and mercy
may speedily help and deliver us;
through Jesus Christ your Son our Lord,
to whom with you and the Holy Spirit,
be honour and glory, now and for ever.

Isaiah 35

This magnificent chapter is one of the great things in Scripture. It offers us a vision of a renewed cosmos that both restores and transcends the opening chapters of Genesis. Here we are not only offered a world in which human beings and animals will live in peace: we are offered one in which the flowers that will appear in desert and wilderness will 'rejoice with joy and singing' (35.2), in which all disability will be taken away (35.5-6) and the era of drought will be ended (35.6-7). Even more important, all God's people will have a goal for their journey through life (35.8), and can look forward one day to living in joy and gladness, at peace with God and one another in the heavenly Jerusalem (35.10).

Is this just empty rhetoric? That depends on us. But the season of Advent is supremely a time to ponder: what kind of new world is God calling us into, and what must we do to prepare for it? What is the Church's vision for a cosmos threatened so acutely by economic and environmental disaster? This chapter offers us a blueprint for that vision; and if we can make it our own, we will not only help God bring it to birth, we will also find we are on our way home.

Almighty God,
purify our hearts and minds,
that when your Son Jesus Christ comes again as
judge and saviour
we may be ready to receive him,
who is our Lord and our God.

COLLECT

Matthew 16.13-end

R. S. Thomas in his poem *Pilgrimages* says this: 'He is such a fast God, always leaving as we arrive.' It is an astonishing insight. As soon as we gain some understanding of who God is, God moves on ahead of us, confounding our conclusions, refusing to be pinned down. 'Do not cling to me' is what Jesus said to Mary Magdalene on the first Easter day. Do not think that human understanding can contain or constrain the mystery of God's presence. Therefore, as soon as Peter comes to his own astonishing conclusion that Jesus is not just a prophet, not just a great man, he is thrown backwards: this Messiah must suffer and die and those who follow him must carry the same cross. In one breath Peter is named as the rock upon which this house will be built; in the other he is revealed as the sand, the stumbling block, even Satan himself, upon which it will crumble. Well might we conclude that there is no profit in gaining this wealth of knowledge if it means losing our soul. So we inch a bit further forward; we ask ourselves again: who can this Christ be? And as we are led into fresh revelations of God's presence, so we are also confronted by our own weakness and need. Like Peter, we are both rock and sand.

COLLECT

O Lord Jesus Christ,
who at your first coming sent your messenger
to prepare your way before you:
grant that the ministers and stewards of your mysteries
may likewise so prepare and make ready your way
by turning the hearts of the disobedient to the wisdom of the just,
that at your second coming to judge the world
we may be found an acceptable people in your sight;
for you are alive and reign with the Father
in the unity of the Holy Spirit,
one God, now and for ever.

Psalms **70**, 74 *or* **48**, 52
Isaiah 38.9-20
Matthew 17.1-13

Matthew 17.1-13

There is a story about a man who dies and goes to heaven but is surprised to find two entrances. Above one door it says 'heaven'. Above the other it says 'interesting discussion about the concept of heaven'. Everyone is queuing up at the second door. The transfiguration of Jesus is a glimpse through the first door: the sign that, ultimately, we are not saved by our own wisdom and understanding but by the astounding generosity and goodness of God. In Christ we see our future. It is not our ideas about God that save us, but God.

Poor Peter, he will continue to struggle, thinking he has to work it out for himself and do it in his own strength. But he and his two companions are given the astonishing gift of the future: an assurance of that ultimate well-being which we have with God. Naturally they want to stay there. They even come up with the lame suggestion of building tents. But what they have received has to be shared. This vision of the journey's end must shape the way they travel.

God for whom we watch and wait,
you sent John the Baptist to prepare the way of your Son:
give us courage to speak the truth,
to hunger for justice,
and to suffer for the cause of right,
with Jesus Christ our Lord.

COLLECT

Matthew 17.14-21

'Your disciples failed', moans the father of the epileptic boy. Jesus is impatient and angry. Those who bring the boy are called faithless and perverse. The demon that possesses the boy is rebuked. The disciples are chastised. They whine to Jesus about their inability to heal the boy. They feign concern, wondering whether Jesus might reveal to them some failsafe technique for healing. But Jesus tells them that all they need is an infinitesimal bit of faith – faith as tiny as a mustard seed. But of course it is not faith they are after, but power. And while they hanker after spiritual clout, they will end up disappointed.

But a little bit of self-emptying faith can move a mountain. However, first of all control must be relinquished. Meanwhile, I live my life demanding my requests be met, craving power and influence, asking for everything except the mustard seed of faith that would make all the difference.

COLLECT

O Lord Jesus Christ,
who at your first coming sent your messenger
to prepare your way before you:
grant that the ministers and stewards of your mysteries
may likewise so prepare and make ready your way
by turning the hearts of the disobedient to the wisdom of the just,
that at your second coming to judge the world
we may be found an acceptable people in your sight;
for you are alive and reign with the Father
in the unity of the Holy Spirit,
one God, now and for ever.

Psalms **46**, 95
Zephaniah 1.1 – 2.3
Matthew 17.22-end

Zephaniah 1.1 – 2.3

The spectre of judgement hangs over Advent. It's not just about preparing for Christmas. It's about preparing to meet God face to face. Zephaniah confronts the scepticism, apostasy and corruption of his day with a sweeping condemnation of all that will befall those who turn from God's ways. You will not live in the houses you build. You will not drink wine from the vineyards you tend. The day of God's wrath is approaching. Ruin and devastation will follow. Zephaniah's words form the basis of the medieval hymn *Dies Irae*, which became part of the liturgy of a requiem mass. It announces God's terrible judgement. The only possible response is fearful silence.

But the judgement that God reveals in Christ warrants a different response. The Christian story, while still assuring us of God's justice, promises that the judge whom God has appointed is Jesus. His birth is a sign of God's solidarity with us. His death is the sign of God's love for us – he will do everything to save us from the consequences of our own bad judgement. His rising again is the sign of our ultimate well-being and acquittal. His coming again is the guarantee that judgement is real – but our response can be one of joyful expectation. Why should I dread the judgement of one who has done so much to save me?

God for whom we watch and wait,
you sent John the Baptist to prepare the way of your Son:
give us courage to speak the truth,
to hunger for justice,
and to suffer for the cause of right,
with Jesus Christ our Lord.

COLLECT

Friday 21 December

Zephaniah 3.1-13

But what of those who turn their face against the mercy of God, who are without trust, who accept no correction, who consciously choose what they know to be wrong, who scorn the advice and pleading of those who call for repentance? Zephaniah rails against those who are eager to make their actions ever more corrupt. They poison the well of their own hearts, and everything that comes out of them is false. They may never be able to acknowledge or receive God's mercy even when it is staring them in the face.

It has been said that God never sends anyone to hell, but some people choose to go there themselves.

And what of me? Lord, temper my pride. Count me as one of those who are lowly and humble in heart, as someone who knows their need of God. Let me seek my refuge in you and save me from allowing the abundance of God's mercy to be assumed with complacency.

COLLECT

O Lord Jesus Christ,
who at your first coming sent your messenger
to prepare your way before you:
grant that the ministers and stewards of your mysteries
may likewise so prepare and make ready your way
by turning the hearts of the disobedient to the wisdom of the just,
that at your second coming to judge the world
we may be found an acceptable people in your sight;
for you are alive and reign with the Father
in the unity of the Holy Spirit,
one God, now and for ever.

Psalms **124**, 125, 126, 127
Zephaniah 3.14-end
Matthew 18.21-end

Zephaniah 3.14-end

Into the confusions of our bad judgement, the paranoia of our fear and the delusions of our misplaced hope, God himself enters with joy. This is the Advent hope: daughter of Zion sing and exult with all your heart, the Lord has taken away all his judgements, the holy one is in your midst. 'The Virgin is with child,' says Isaiah, 'and will bear a son and you will name him Emmanuel.' This is the Christmas message: God is with us – the basis of our hope and the source of our deliverance. God will remove every disaster and restore all our fortunes. It won't be as we expect or according to our schedules. But it will be glorious. The writs against us will be torn up. The pleadings of our heart will be answered. We will behold and receive God in the only language we really understand: the language of another human life.

And this will be challenging. God will be just as forgiving with those who have hurt me as with those I have hurt. God will ask me to hold them and help them. God will bring everything into light. Like an artist patiently bringing to completion the emerging portrait on the canvas, God will work on me. God is becoming what we are so that we can know and receive what God is.

God for whom we watch and wait,
you sent John the Baptist to prepare the way of your Son:
give us courage to speak the truth,
to hunger for justice,
and to suffer for the cause of right,
with Jesus Christ our Lord.

COLLECT

19

Monday 24 December

Christmas Eve

Malachi 1.1,6-end

'I will not accept an offering from your hands', says the Lord through the prophet Malachi. 'You wouldn't fob off your earthly governor with the diseased offerings you bring to me. I can only conclude that you despise me.' With these terrible words it seems as if access to God is closed down. All the hopes of the Old Testament have come to nothing. We simply aren't able to make the offering that God desires. Everything that we could offer falls short.

In the book of Genesis, Abraham is given the terrible job of sacrificing his own son. It is a strange and disturbing story. But it ends with God's reprieve. Isaac is spared and Abraham hears the promise that God will personally provide a lamb for the slaughter. At that moment Abraham spies a ram caught in a thicket and believes this is what God means. But now we fast forward to the stable in Bethlehem, to shepherds arriving with lambs on their shoulders, and to the terrible words of John the Baptist when he first sees Christ: 'Behold the Lamb of God.' The child whose birth we celebrate tonight – the one whose birth-day present is myrrh for burial – he is the one who will freely and generously offer his unblemished life of perfect love so that all the children of God can be spared.

COLLECT

Almighty God,
you make us glad with the yearly remembrance
of the birth of your Son Jesus Christ:
grant that, as we joyfully receive him as our redeemer,
so we may with sure confidence behold him
when he shall come to be our judge;
who is alive and reigns with you,
in the unity of the Holy Spirit,
one God, now and for ever.

Psalms **110**, 117
Isaiah 62.1-5
Matthew 1.18-25

Matthew 1.18-25

Today we give thanks for the faithfulness of Mary. She responded to God's call with clarity and joy. But what about Joseph? What did he have to go on? Mary had the evidence of the child growing in her womb. Joseph only had a dream. Yet, his faithfulness to the dream and his steadfast love for Mary create the space where Jesus is born.

So Joseph can encourage us to listen to our dreams. He can shame us into trusting those we love. He can stiffen our resolve to go where we are led. This is enormously hard. Maybe it takes a dream and a vision to pluck up the courage.

So what is our vision? What is our dream? Looking into the manger we see the enormity of God's self-emptying love. This is how far God reaches to pick us up. But in Christ we are also asked to pick God up! We experience God in a way that shatters illusions and reconstructs dreams – for to hold the baby Jesus in your hands as Mary and Joseph did is to hold God.

Mary is told to name him Emmanuel, 'God with us'. That was her experience. Joseph is told he will be Jesus, 'God saves'. Perhaps that was the vision that sustained him. For us, he will be both.

> Almighty God,
> you have given us your only-begotten Son
> to take our nature upon him
> and as at this time to be born of a pure virgin:
> grant that we, who have been born again
> and made your children by adoption and grace,
> may daily be renewed by your Holy Spirit;
> through Jesus Christ your Son our Lord,
> who is alive and reigns with you,
> in the unity of the Holy Spirit,
> one God, now and for ever.

COLLECT

21

Wednesday 26 December

Stephen, deacon and martyr

Psalms **13**, 31.1-8, 150
Jeremiah 26.12-15
Acts 6

Acts 6

The Christian calendar doesn't let us stay at Bethlehem for long. We move swiftly from birth to death and celebrate the Church's first martyr. So don't get sentimental about Christmas. And don't hang about this stable if you want an easy life.

Stephen shows us where following Christ leads. No sooner has he been appointed to wait at tables and look after the widows than he has gone AWOL and is preaching to the Sanhedrin and getting himself killed. The cleansing water of faith leads to the hot water of controversy. So much for a New Testament pattern of ministry! The only thing we learn here is that the Holy Spirit is in charge.

Christ's birth, death and resurrection change everything. We no longer need to rely on creed, cult or conduct to be OK with God. We no longer need to depend on temples made by human hands. Jesus is the one in whom we worship; in him we have access to God.

And Stephen, the one who dies because he worships God through Jesus, appears before his accusers with the face of an angel. For as St Paul tells us, it is with our unveiled faces, reflecting the glory we see, that we are changed (2 Corinthians 3.18). As W. H. Auden wrote: 'The blessed will not care what angle they are regarded from, having nothing to hide.'

COLLECT

Gracious Father,
who gave the first martyr Stephen
grace to pray for those who took up stones against him:
grant that in all our sufferings for the truth
we may learn to love even our enemies
and seek forgiveness for those who desire our hurt,
looking up to heaven to him who was crucified for us,
Jesus Christ, our mediator and advocate,
who is alive and reigns with you,
in the unity of the Holy Spirit,
one God, now and for ever.

Psalms **21**, 147.13-end
Exodus 33.12-23
1 John 2.1-11

John, apostle and evangelist

1 John 2.1-11

The love of God changes everything. Now we are invited to see everything in the light that is Christ. And it is not so much that God lives in us – though he does – it is that we live in him, our hearts and minds are conformed to his: because we abide in Christ we must walk as he walked.

And just about the hardest bit of this is loving your neighbour. It is relatively easy to love people you don't see very often, or allow yourself to have all kinds of good and charitable thoughts about people far away and even – now and again – to do some good towards them. But loving the person next to you ... loving the very particular, not apparently very loveable, prickly and opinionated person who is with you now, this is altogether different. It is so very easy to end up talking about the light and yet walking in the darkness. We won't be judged by our eloquent espousals of the Christian life, but by our actions. Did we, or did we not, love our neighbour?

Merciful Lord,
cast your bright beams of light upon the Church:
that, being enlightened by the teaching
of your blessed apostle and evangelist Saint John,
we may so walk in the light of your truth
that we may at last attain to the light of everlasting life;
through Jesus Christ your incarnate Son our Lord,
who is alive and reigns with you,
in the unity of the Holy Spirit,
one God, now and for ever.

COLLECT

23

Friday 28 December

The Holy Innocents

Psalms **36**, 146
Baruch 4.21-27 *or* Genesis 37.13-20
Matthew 18.1-10

Matthew 18.1-10

It is hard to read these words of Jesus on the day the Church remembers the massacre of the innocents. But this again is where following Christ leads. For those whose hearts are ruled by darkness, the sheer loveliness of Christ is abhorrent and threatening and to be stamped out. Herod, in a murderous rage, spills the blood of many children and Jerusalem laments again. How hard it is to read these words in our own day knowing that in Palestine and across the troubled lands of the Middle East many innocents are slaughtered and many mothers weep.

How can we respond? Well, we must listen to Jesus who tells us that the best antidote to the darkness of murderous envy is child-like joy. And turning on its head all the proud expectations of the world, he puts a little child in the middle and says that if you want to enter God's kingdom (and of course many people don't!) then this is how you must become. This is the challenge: become like a child, trusting and full of hope; receive each other as a child, and cut out from your life all that would crave power and control. For a child knows its need of resources beyond itself. And adults tend to think they are in charge.

COLLECT

Heavenly Father,
whose children suffered at the hands of Herod,
though they had done no wrong:
by the suffering of your Son
and by the innocence of our lives
frustrate all evil designs
and establish your reign of justice and peace;
through Jesus Christ your Son our Lord,
who is alive and reigns with you,
in the unity of the Holy Spirit,
one God, now and for ever.

Psalms **19**, 20
Jonah 1
Colossians 1.1-14

Colossians 1.1-14

Children's prayers usually begin with the words 'thank you'. Adults' prayers usually begin with the word 'please'. But if we dwell in God's kingdom, we should all live with child-like thanksgiving. Hence, Paul's letters always begin and end with thanks. Indeed, we use the Greek word for thanksgiving – Eucharist – as the name for the central act of Christian worship. And it is a thanksgiving that goes on even when we face challenge and suffering. It is the joyful refusal to submit to the pessimism and defeat of the world. 'Endure everything with patience,' says Paul, 'give thanks to God.'

Paul rejoices that this hope has taken root in the church at Colossae, and beginning his letter to them he calls them 'saints'. Now we usually reserve this word for the most holy and distinguished Christians. But the journey of Advent and Christmas indicates a deeper truth – that all of us are saints: not because of our goodness or even our holiness (this is not the point), but because of what God has done in Christ and because we have responded. We have received the gift of a new life and we have found ourselves re-created and re-focused in Christ. We are holy – we are saints – because we now live our lives in union with a holy God. Worth a 'thank you', don't you think?

Lord Jesus Christ,
your birth at Bethlehem
draws us to kneel in wonder at heaven touching earth:
accept our heartfelt praise
as we worship you,
our Saviour and our eternal God.

COLLECT

Monday 31 December

Colossians 1.24 – 2.7

Secrets are alluring. We learn from an early age the delight of keeping things hidden from others and the frustration that arises when others keep things hidden from us. Sometimes religion can feel like an advanced version of these early secrets: there are mysteries that are hidden from us which only the most committed, the most exceptional, the most chosen will uncover. There is something about the human psyche that revels in mystery, in the feeling that if only we try hard enough, we will uncover the greatest secret of all. It is this quest that has driven people down the ages to seek for the Holy Grail, the Lost Ark, or the tomb of Jesus.

The irony is that God has no desire at all to keep things from us but yearns to pour out the riches of heaven. The wonder of the Christian message is that, in Christ, God has already made the innermost secrets of heaven available to everyone who believes. There is no secret, only the unbounded depth of God's generous self, made ready for each one of us. There is nothing hidden, simply plenty that we cannot comprehend – in the words of Walter C. Smith's famous hymn, ''Tis only the splendour of light hideth thee'.

COLLECT

Almighty God,
who wonderfully created us in your own image
and yet more wonderfully restored us
through your Son Jesus Christ:
grant that, as he came to share in our humanity,
so we may share the life of his divinity;
who is alive and reigns with you,
in the unity of the Holy Spirit,
one God, now and for ever.

26

Psalms **103**, 150
Genesis 17.1-13
Romans 2.17-29

The Naming and Circumcision of Jesus

Romans 2.17-29

One of the most beautiful images of the Gospel narratives is that evoked first by Simeon, cradling the tiny Christ-child, then by Anna, offering homage to the one who brought life, as their own lives ebbed slowly away (Luke chapter 2). Woven into this picture is a reminder of the deeply Jewish origins of our faith. This story celebrates Jesus' membership of God's historic covenant people through his circumcision in the temple.

In his life and ministry, Jesus became the epitome of what Paul was calling for in Romans 2.17-29. Jesus' teaching was powerful, not just because of the words he used, but also because of the life he lived; Jesus joyfully, faithfully, compassionately lived out his covenant membership in humble obedience to God's commands. The power of Jesus' life came from his integrity, an integrity that fulfilled to overflowing God's covenant with his people and showed what it meant to obey the law in deed as well as word. Yet, in the mysterious and paradoxical ways of God, it was his perfect fulfilling of the law that marked a movement away from old to new, from law to grace and faith. The start of this movement began, at least in part, with this moment of cradling and recognition that took place at Jesus' circumcision.

Almighty God,
whose blessed Son was circumcised
in obedience to the law for our sake
and given the Name that is above every name:
give us grace faithfully to bear his Name,
to worship him in the freedom of the Spirit,
and to proclaim him as the Saviour of the world;
who is alive and reigns with you,
in the unity of the Holy Spirit,
one God, now and for ever.

COLLECT

27

Wednesday 2 January

Colossians 2.8-end

Freedom is something we all yearn for, and yet struggle to accept. Soon after they left Egypt, the Israelites became nostalgic for the good old days, when they had food to eat and water to drink. They might have been physically free, but mentally and emotionally they were still in slavery. The Colossians seem to have been the same. They had accepted the freedom offered to them in Christ; they had died and risen through baptism and they had left behind the old and embraced the new. What did they then do to celebrate this freedom in Christ? They allowed themselves to be bossed around by those with strong views on eating, drinking and worshipping.

You cannot make someone free simply by opening the door. True freedom, the kind of freedom that God longs to give, cannot happen overnight. This freedom involves the freeing of our whole self – mind, body and spirit. In his death and resurrection, Christ opened the door, but to gain true freedom we have not only to step through it, but to stay there. Accepting freedom involves giving up what we know and embracing a new future. That can be harder than many of us dare to think.

COLLECT

Almighty God,
who wonderfully created us in your own image
and yet more wonderfully restored us
through your Son Jesus Christ:
grant that, as he came to share in our humanity,
so we may share the life of his divinity;
who is alive and reigns with you,
in the unity of the Holy Spirit,
one God, now and for ever.

Psalms **127**, 128, 131
Ruth 2
Colossians 3.1-11

Colossians 3.1-11

Imagine a lavish party. The room is beautifully decorated; a sumptuous feast is laid out; the guests have all arrived wearing their most glamorous clothes. Finally, the guest of honour is announced and appears in the doorway, dirty from the garden, wearing her oldest, most worn clothes, which are covered in stains and reeking of all sorts of bad smells. Being in Christ but not acting as though we are, is to turn up to God's feast badly dressed and unwashed.

Of course, this does not mean that transforming our actions from the old self to the new is easy. If only it were. It would be a great relief if, once we were 'in Christ', all our desires to act badly miraculously disappeared. Sadly, the opposite seems to be the case; knowing you shouldn't do it – and shouldn't even *want* to do it – somehow makes the desire to act badly even stronger. Nevertheless, we should strive to put to death the old self and fill our minds to the brim with 'things that are above'. If our minds are full of the new, there is less room for the old, so that, with time, the clothes of our new self replace the old. Then we can be guests of God, not only welcome at the feast, but dressed properly too.

God in Trinity,
eternal unity of perfect love:
gather the nations to be one family,
and draw us into your holy life
through the birth of Emmanuel,
our Lord Jesus Christ.

COLLECT

Friday 4 January	Psalm **89.1-37** Ruth 3 Colossians 3.12 – 4.1

Colossians 3.12 – 4.1

What is the difference between a saint and a doormat? This sounds like the opening line of a joke, but it isn't – it is a serious question. The attitude and character of God's holy and beloved elect, outlined here, teeter on the brink of behaviour so subservient and self-denying that it might appear weak and insubstantial. However, anyone who has had the privilege of knowing a true saint – by which I mean someone from whom the love of God shines forth for all to see – would be able to tell you that there is a world of difference between a saint and someone who is so subservient that they refuse to stand up to anyone. So what is that difference?

On the surface, being a 'saint' does require meek and mild behaviour – compassion, kindness, humility, meekness, patience, being endlessly forgiving and loving. The difference between the two, however, lies not on the surface, but far below in the depths of our being. The kind of attitude that Paul is calling for here comes not from vapid indecision, but from the peace of Christ reigning in our hearts and the word of Christ dwelling in us richly. Action which arises from such roots will be far from insipid – you only have to look at Jesus to see that.

COLLECT

Almighty God,
who wonderfully created us in your own image
and yet more wonderfully restored us
through your Son Jesus Christ:
grant that, as he came to share in our humanity,
so we may share the life of his divinity;
who is alive and reigns with you,
in the unity of the Holy Spirit,
one God, now and for ever.

Colossians 4.2-end

Not long ago I was talking to someone who was a relatively new churchgoer. She was frankly bemused by prayer: 'What is everyone doing,' she asked, 'when they're kneeling down? How will I know if I'm doing it right?' This sense of anxiety about prayer is not reserved for newcomers to church. We can even find it reflected in the disciples' request to Jesus in Luke 11.1 to 'teach them to pray'.

So how should we pray? Colossians tells us that we should 'keep close company with prayer' (the word translated by the NRSV and NIV as 'devote'); it should become our best friend. In other words, quantity rather than quality is important. With our friends we don't wait for a single, perfectly-worded sentence that will sum up the totality of our feeling about something. We talk, we explore ideas, we say how we feel – this is what our prayer life should be like. While we are doing this, we should also keep watch (the same word is used here for what the disciples failed to do in the garden of Gethsemane) in thanksgiving (v. 2) and pray for others (v. 3). In short, the mystery of prayer is not that mysterious after all – the question is not whether we are doing it right, but whether we are doing it at all.

God in Trinity,
eternal unity of perfect love:
gather the nations to be one family,
and draw us into your holy life
through the birth of Emmanuel,
our Lord Jesus Christ.

COLLECT

31

Monday 7 January

Psalms **99**, 147.1-12 *or* **71**
Baruch 1.15 – 2.10 *or* Jeremiah 23.1-8
Matthew 20.1-16

Matthew 20.1-16

'That's not fair!' is a cry that is never far from the lips of children. From an early age we develop a strong sense of what is fair and what is not. Once we grow up, we may not utter the cry quite so readily, but we still think it.

This parable shakes our sense of what is fair and what is not. Our innate sense of fairness dictates that the longer you work the more you are paid. Not so, says Jesus in this parable. The kingdom of heaven is not concerned with detailed accounting, with the careful counting-out of what is owed to whom. It is concerned with ridiculous acts of generosity. God's concern is to lavish good gifts on everyone.

In fact, the fairness of the kingdom of heaven suggests that our fairness is not fairness at all, because it is driven by concern that we should get what we are owed, and that some should get more and some less. The fairness of the kingdom of heaven dictates that everyone receives from the bounty of God. What we receive may not be more than our neighbour, but it will be enough for our needs and, in any case, is very much more than we are owed.

COLLECT

O God,
who by the leading of a star
manifested your only Son to the peoples of the earth:
mercifully grant that we,
who know you now by faith,
may at last behold your glory face to face;
through Jesus Christ your Son our Lord,
who is alive and reigns with you,
in the unity of the Holy Spirit,
one God, now and for ever.

Psalms **46**, 147.13-end *or* **73**
Baruch 2.11-end *or* Jeremiah 30.1-17
Matthew 20.17-28

Tuesday 8 January

Matthew 20.17-28

'Be careful what you wish for, lest it come true' is one of the sayings of our age. We find it wherever we turn – in songs, in headlines and in books. The implication is that we should limit our dreams, squash our hopes into smaller, more containable desires whose consequences may be less frightening and more manageable.

If this saying had been around at the time of Jesus, would he have said it to the mother of James and John when she came to him to ask whether they could sit at his right and left? I suspect not. Jesus does not berate James and John for their mother's request, he simply asks whether they know what they are asking for. Jesus, it seems, does not want us to limit our dreams, but asks us to be prepared to live with the consequences of them. As James and John discovered, following Jesus is never what you expect it to be; the glory of Jesus' kingdom, which they hoped for, was found in death. When we follow Jesus, the consequences of our dreams turn out to be a world away from what we think they will be. Jesus does not caution us against the dreaming – he simply asks whether we are prepared to live with what happens.

Creator of the heavens,
who led the Magi by a star
to worship the Christ-child:
guide and sustain us,
that we may find our journey's end
in Jesus Christ our Lord.

COLLECT

Matthew 20.29-end

The unease in this story is almost palpable. It seems that people who shout were no more welcome during the time of Jesus than they are now. People who shout ignore the rules of polite society; they ruffle our feathers and make us feel uncomfortable. The crowd seem desperate to prevent these two blind men from making a scene and disturbing their day, but Jesus was not driven by similar concerns of etiquette; his concern was motivated not by the demands of politeness but of need. He did not chastise the blind men for making a noise but asked them what they wanted. In fact, it was Jesus' response that allowed the blind men to articulate their need and to find healing.

When people are unruly, our natural response is to shy away, to pretend they haven't spoken and to continue on our way unruffled and undisturbed. The way of the gospel demands a different response. It demands that we stop. It demands that we listen. It demands that we encourage those who shout to identify their need and most of all to respond with compassion when they do. The way of the gospel demands that we place need above politeness, compassion above personal comfort, and careful listening above our desire to quieten those who make us uneasy.

COLLECT

O God,
who by the leading of a star
manifested your only Son to the peoples of the earth:
mercifully grant that we,
who know you now by faith,
may at last behold your glory face to face;
through Jesus Christ your Son our Lord,
who is alive and reigns with you,
in the unity of the Holy Spirit,
one God, now and for ever.

Psalms 97, **149** *or* **78.1-39**
Baruch 3.9 – 4.4 *or* Jeremiah 31.10-17
Matthew 23.1-12

Matthew 23.1-12

Where does the saying 'Do as I say and not as I do' come from? No one is quite sure. Its roots are probably buried so deep in human behaviour that it is hard to tell who first said it. A version of it appears here in Matthew's Gospel: you should do as the Pharisees say but not as they do. Jesus, it appears, subscribes to this as a principle. But how can this be? Surely the principle of saying one thing and doing another is an anathema within Jesus' teaching? This is indeed true; elsewhere in the Gospels we find strong teaching about being people of integrity whose actions flow out of the core of our being.

Here, Jesus means something else. He is not talking about how we should act, but about how we should react to what others do and say. We need to be people of discernment. His hearers may wish, correctly, to reject the excesses and corruption that Jesus lists, but they should take care lest they also throw out the teaching that underpins it. There is nothing wrong, Jesus tells us, with the teaching, only with the way in which it is being carried out. Jesus calls for us to be people who can not only resist falsehood but also discern truth, even if the two are woven together.

Creator of the heavens,
who led the Magi by a star
to worship the Christ-child:
guide and sustain us,
that we may find our journey's end
in Jesus Christ our Lord.

COLLECT

Matthew 23.13-28

'Mild, obedient, good as he': only a few weeks ago churches across the country were ringing with these words in praise of Jesus' gentleness, as penned by Cecil Frances Alexander in 'Once in Royal David's City'. Anyone reading today's passage might be forgiven for wondering where this mild, passive human being had gone to. Here, Jesus' blisteringly angry words rise from the page, searing us with the extent and depth of his anger. This is no gentle Jesus, meek and mild. This is raging Jesus, furious and in full swing.

The Jesus we meet in the Gospels is far from the gentle and mild figure of Victorian portrayals. The Jesus of the Gospels rages against corruption, hypocrisy and injustice. He fumes against those whose practice of religion thwarts people's search for God. He rants against a religion whose concern with the minutiae of worship prevents others from grasping the truth. This Jesus challenges our apathy and calls us to be fellow 'ragers' for the kingdom. At the same time, he dares us to look deeply at our own religious practices and to ask whether our rage should really begin at home.

COLLECT

O God,
who by the leading of a star
manifested your only Son to the peoples of the earth:
mercifully grant that we,
who know you now by faith,
may at last behold your glory face to face;
through Jesus Christ your Son our Lord,
who is alive and reigns with you,
in the unity of the Holy Spirit,
one God, now and for ever.

Psalms **96**, 145 *or* **76**, 79
Baruch 4.36 – 5.end *or* Micah 5.2-end
Matthew 23.29-end

Matthew 23.29-end

One of my favourite churches around Jerusalem is Dominus Flevit, otherwise known as the 'teardrop church'. As its name suggests, the building is shaped like a teardrop, and the view from inside, through the wide window that stands behind the altar, is of Jerusalem spread out below. The altar frontal portrays a mosaic of a hen, wings spread out, brooding over her chicks. The very ordering of the church invites you to sit and brood, as Jesus did, over a city as torn now by violence and strife as it was when Jesus brooded over it two thousand years ago.

Verse 37, so powerfully symbolized in Dominus Flevit, gives us a brief insight into the heart of God: a heart that yearns to gather humankind close and yet recognizes that true love involves freedom, the freedom to reject as well as to accept love. It invites us to brood with God over Jerusalem and all those war-torn cities and lands whose very conflict blinds them to the path of love. It invites us to recognize that sometimes all we can do is yearn for those who cannot find their way into God's love but, most of all, it reminds us that a place exists for each one of us beneath God's mothering wing, if only we are willing.

Creator of the heavens,
who led the Magi by a star
to worship the Christ-child:
guide and sustain us,
that we may find our journey's end
in Jesus Christ our Lord.

COLLECT

Psalms **2**, 110 *or* **80**, 82
Genesis 1.1-19
Matthew 21.1-17

Genesis 1.1-19

The Bible opens with a picture of God and nothingness. As something comes to be where once there was nothing, the first thing the universe knows is the voice of God. Although there is no created thing to hear, yet God speaks. Human beings will learn that words, and all that they will come to symbolize about communication and relationship, are dear to God. But the God we see at the beginning of the world communicates not just with human creation but with everything that is made. God's voice, God's breath, God's ideas and imagination, activate all existence, not just ours.

The Bible begins here, not just because it is logical to start at the beginning. When the book of Genesis comes into its final written form, in about the sixth century BC, God's people, Israel, are in exile, and all their hopes are in tatters. They might have been tempted to think that their God had been defeated by others. But Genesis reminds them that there are no others. This is the God who calls creation out of nothing and whose creativity is inexhaustible.

COLLECT

Eternal Father,
Who at the baptism of Jesus
revealed him to be your Son,
anointing him with the Holy Spirit:
grant to us who are born again by water and the Spirit,
that we may be faithful to our calling as your adopted children;
through Jesus Christ your Son our Lord,
who is alive and reigns with you,
in the unity of the Holy Spirit,
one God, now and for ever.

Psalms 8, **9** *or* 87, **89.1-18**
Genesis 1.20 – 2.3
Matthew 21.18-32

Genesis 1.20 – 2.3

God is an exuberant creator. This passage teems with life and sound. Before verse 20, the only sound is God speaking into the beautiful space he has made out of nothingness. But now God's creatures begin to reply, with squeaks, squawks, splashes, grunts, and God loves it. Every creature is born with God's blessing, knowing itself to be a source of joy to God.

At each point, as creation progresses from one state to another, God could have stopped. We, with bitter hindsight, long to call out to him, 'Quit while you're ahead, God! Just look at the sky, sea and earth, lit by sun and moon, and enjoy the exquisite landscape. Or just play with the birds, sea monsters and animals you've made. Playing with your lovely pets is much safer than making human beings!' But God is bolder than us. God does make people. He makes them like himself, so that the created world will recognize God's image in them. Although sharing God's creativity is an awesome responsibility, it is first of all a joy, the joy we see as God makes all things.

Heavenly Father,
at the Jordan you revealed Jesus as your Son:
may we recognize him as our Lord
and know ourselves to be your beloved children;
through Jesus Christ our Saviour.

COLLECT

Wednesday 16 January

Psalms 19, **20** or 119.105-128
Genesis 2.4-end
Matthew 21.33-end

Genesis 2.4-end

God sits like a child on the ground, making mud pies. Perhaps we do not like to think of ourselves as God's mud pies but, actually, there is an extraordinary tenderness and intimacy in this picture. It is very physical; God's hands pummel us into shape and then God's breath fills us. Then, all around the clay figures, God makes a garden.

The garden is not all that exists. It is given a location in a bigger world. It is 'in the east', and it shares a river, a life source, with the world outside the garden. So this is not really a creation story, like Genesis 1. It is designed to make us think about the origins of our separation from God, all the more heart-breaking as we see the ease and friendliness between God and his 'clay people' here at the start. The 'tree of the knowledge of good and evil' is not some magical thing with the power to reveal what is hidden, but a choice we make, something that brings into being what is not there before – a will different from God's.

COLLECT

Eternal Father,
Who at the baptism of Jesus
revealed him to be your Son,
anointing him with the Holy Spirit:
grant to us who are born again by water and the Spirit,
that we may be faithful to our calling as your adopted children;
through Jesus Christ your Son our Lord,
who is alive and reigns with you,
in the unity of the Holy Spirit,
one God, now and for ever.

Psalms **21**, 24 *or* 90, **92**
Genesis 3
Matthew 22.1-14

Genesis 3

It is terribly hard to read this passage without preconceptions. So much theology depends on this one chapter, and it has been reworked so many times, in sermons, in literature, in the whole Christian psyche.

We all know, for example, that the serpent is 'evil', don't we, and then wonder how evil can exist before the first sin has been committed? But actually, the story only says that the serpent is 'subtle'. The ingenious word-game it plays with the woman could have been mere mischievous showing-off, if the woman had responded differently. She and the man are supposed to share God's care for the other creatures, so when she follows the serpent's advice instead of her own knowledge of God, she is disturbing the proper order of things. The result is that the relations between God, humans and the rest of creation will now be out of joint. The intimacy between God and people will be lost, as will the easy relationship of trust and nurture between people and the non-human creation. The voice of God, which drew creation out of nothing, is now calling, through eternity, to the people he has made, calling them back to the intimacy they have lost.

Heavenly Father,
at the Jordan you revealed Jesus as your Son:
may we recognize him as our Lord
and know ourselves to be your beloved children;
through Jesus Christ our Saviour.

COLLECT

Friday 18 January

Psalms **67**, 72 *or* **88**, 95
Genesis 4.1-16,25-26
Matthew 22.15-33

Genesis 4.1-16,25-26

Although Adam and Eve can never return to Eden, yet they do not forget their God. Even if they can no longer walk and talk with him in the cool of the evening, God is still the whole horizon of what they and their children do. In particular, they automatically connect anything creative they do with God, whether it is producing a child, growing a crop or taking care of the sheep.

We don't know why God prefers Abel's offering to Cain's. But it is Cain, not God, who sees that as a rejection. God tells Cain that he is still perfectly accepted and loved, even though his offering is not chosen. Even after the murder of Abel, God puts his mark on Cain, not to alert people to his wickedness, but to protect him. It is something in us that cannot believe we are loved unless we are centre stage. We childishly believe that unless we are the chosen ones, we are rejected, as though those are the only two options. But that is not how God works. God's chosen people are always a means to include others, not exclude them. The mark of Cain on the foreheads of those who feel rejected is really a sign of God's patience and care, as he waits to bring them home.

COLLECT

Eternal Father,
Who at the baptism of Jesus
revealed him to be your Son,
anointing him with the Holy Spirit:
grant to us who are born again by water and the Spirit,
that we may be faithful to our calling as your adopted children;
through Jesus Christ your Son our Lord,
who is alive and reigns with you,
in the unity of the Holy Spirit,
one God, now and for ever.

Psalms 29, **33** *or* 96, **97**, 100
Genesis 6.1-10
Matthew 22.34-end

Genesis 6.1-10

This is a very strange little passage, with clear echoes in Middle Eastern mythology. There were legends of a tribe of giants, who were supposed to have been produced by a union between human women and divine beings. In fact, Numbers 13.33 mentions the Nephilim again, as the tribe of huge beings that Moses and the people must conquer before they can enter the Land.

But this passage is only incidentally about the Nephilim. In Genesis, they are not given divine status, but something between humanity and God. Whatever they are, they are not blamed for what is to come. The sinfulness that is going to cause God such anger is laid squarely at the feet of human beings. Yet again, as in Genesis 2 – 3, human beings are failing to observe the created order. They are trying to be like gods, again, and blur the boundaries between human and divine responsibilities. They have forgotten that they are not in charge of the world, and believe they can act with total autonomy. But God the creator has bound the fate of humans and the fate of the world together in his great creative act. We forget it at our peril.

Heavenly Father,
at the Jordan you revealed Jesus as your Son:
may we recognize him as our Lord
and know ourselves to be your beloved children;
through Jesus Christ our Saviour.

COLLECT

Monday 21 January

Psalms 145, **146** *or* **98**, 99, 101
Genesis 6.11 – 7.10
Matthew 24.1-14

Genesis 6.11 – 7.10

At the heart of the story of Noah's ark is a great paradox. On the one hand, we are told that God is so angry that he proposes to destroy the world. On the other hand, we see God acting with great care to preserve what he has made. God's instructions to Noah are precise and detailed – designed to ensure that what emerges after the flood is continuous with what went before. Odd behaviour from a destructive deity?

Yet this paradox is one of the identifying characteristics of the God of the Bible. 'Hatred' and 'anger' are the only human words we can find to express God's attitude to sin. But while human hatred and anger are always destructive, God's hatred and anger renew. When Israel is decimated and exiled, what emerges is a people as numerous as the stars in the sky. When Jesus is crucified, his resurrection provides life for the world. When Christians are baptized, destroying our old lives in the flood water, we are reborn into the new life of Christ. None of this is without pain, but it is the extraordinary fruit of the creative anger of God.

COLLECT

Almighty God,
whose Son revealed in signs and miracles
the wonder of your saving presence:
renew your people with your heavenly grace,
and in all our weakness
sustain us by your mighty power;
through Jesus Christ your Son our Lord,
who is alive and reigns with you,
in the unity of the Holy Spirit,
one God, now and for ever.

Psalms **132**, 147.1-12 *or* **106** *or* 103
Genesis 7.11-end
Matthew 24.15-28

Genesis 7.11-end

Irresistibly, our imaginations people the ark. We tell stories about Noah and his family, their squabbles, their joys and struggles. We imagine the animals, in their fetid and overcrowded conditions, forced to live closely together and to adjust to each other. In the Garden of Eden, they were used to this, but they, like human beings, have learned different ways since those days.

But the Genesis account is focused outside the ark, not inside. The authors of Genesis do not concentrate on the tiny, frail boat, tossing on the water, with its valiant and comic cargo. Instead, they see the waters of chaos overwhelming the creation, rushing back into their original possession of all that is. God made space for creation by giving the mighty water boundaries, which it obediently and meekly respected. It was the human creation that transgressed the limits God laid out, and now they see what happens when creation breaks out of its proper course. Everything God made in Genesis 1 is interdependent, designed to function as a whole. That is its strength. When it forgets that, how very fragile it is. Only God exists in complete freedom and autonomy. The waters of chaos do not care about their drowned cargo. In that, they represent us, when we forget what we are.

God of all mercy,
your Son proclaimed good news to the poor,
release to the captives,
and freedom to the oppressed:
anoint us with your Holy Spirit
and set all your people free
to praise you in Christ our Lord.

COLLECT

Wednesday 23 January

Psalms **81**, 147.13-end
or 110, **111**, 112
Genesis 8.1-14
Matthew 24.29-end

Genesis 8.1-14

There has been a lot of forgetting in the story so far. Human beings forgot that they were made to be with God and share his care of creation. They forgot that they were not independent and god-like beings, but creatures. The waters forgot the boundaries that God had set for them, and thundered back over creation. The living things, drowning helplessly in the indifferent, violent strength of the waters, forgot everything in the deep darkness of death. It is as though the universe had forgotten that there had ever been a creation, now that there is only formless void and empty waters again. The tiny bobbing craft, carrying all that remains of creation, is utterly forgotten by the elements.

But God remembers. God's 'remembering' is one of the ways in which the Bible describes God's faithfulness, while emphasizing that God is faithful because he chooses to be, not because we have rights over him. God 'remembers' his promises to Abraham and Isaac; he 'remembers' his covenant with David; and now, he 'remembers' the ark and its contents, and replays his first creative acts, restraining the waters and making room for the hospitable ground again. When we 'remember' Jesus, in the Eucharist, we are trusting ourselves to God's remembering, which brings new life out of the grave.

COLLECT

Almighty God,
whose Son revealed in signs and miracles
the wonder of your saving presence:
renew your people with your heavenly grace,
and in all our weakness
sustain us by your mighty power;
through Jesus Christ your Son our Lord,
who is alive and reigns with you,
in the unity of the Holy Spirit,
one God, now and for ever.

Psalms **76**, 148 *or* 113, **115**
Genesis 8.15 – 9.7
Matthew 25.1-13

Genesis 8.15 – 9.7

Although there is real continuity between the world before and after the Flood, some things have changed for ever. The boundaries between God and people, and people and the rest of creation have shifted significantly. So as Noah steps out onto the dry land, he builds the first altar and offers the first animal sacrifice.

In Genesis 2 and 3, God and people talk without reserve. Adam and Eve are vegetarians, who can eat anything that grows, but not the animals. In Genesis 4, the first innocent blood is shed when Cain kills Abel, and by the end of the chapter, people learn how to pray to God. This is not wrong, but it marks another stage. Now, after the devastating death and destruction of the waters, things have changed again. People no longer just care for the animals, they also use them, to feed themselves and to offer to God. Violence and the possibility of misunderstanding have crept into all created relationships, which can now only be maintained at a cost.

Genesis does not encourage nostalgia. We cannot get back to the Garden. Things are as they are. But Jesus' death and our sacramental re-enactment of it is about God's transformation of our violent impulses. By sacrificing himself, Jesus forces even death to acknowledge the creativity of God.

God of all mercy,
your Son proclaimed good news to the poor,
release to the captives,
and freedom to the oppressed:
anoint us with your Holy Spirit
and set all your people free
to praise you in Christ our Lord.

COLLECT

Friday 25 January

The Conversion of Paul

Psalms **27**, 149 *or* **139**
Genesis 9.8-19
Matthew 25.14-30

Genesis 9.8-19

A covenant was a legally binding agreement between two parties, before witnesses and with penalties imposed if either side broke the promise.

*Readings for the
Conversion of Paul*
Psalms 66, 147.13-21
Ezekiel 3.22-27
Philippians 3.1-14
Colossians 1.24 – 2.7

So it is an odd word for God to use here. Noah is not promising anything, nor is he forfeiting anything. God, on the other hand, is promising to restrain his own divine powers and bind himself to his creatures. He is forfeiting his right to unmake what he has made. So God deliberately allows himself and his creation to be vulnerable to these human beings. He binds his own hands, while leaving Noah and his descendants free. They still bear the image of God, and they are still free to multiply and take over God's world (see Genesis 9.6-7), but God is no longer free to unloose the waters of chaos again. He has made a solemn covenant.

God's covenant with Noah is automatically a covenant with all other living creatures, not just human beings, because the image of God in humanity still binds them together with the animals that God brought to meet Adam in Genesis 2. Human beings may not always recognize this connection, but the rest of creation knows it, often to its cost.

COLLECT

Almighty God,
who caused the light of the gospel
to shine throughout the world
through the preaching of your servant Saint Paul:
grant that we who celebrate his wonderful conversion
may follow him in bearing witness to your truth;
through Jesus Christ your Son our Lord,
who is alive and reigns with you,
in the unity of the Holy Spirit,
one God, now and for ever.

Psalms **122**, 128, 150 *or* 120, **121**, 122
Genesis 11.1-9
Matthew 25.31-end

Genesis 11.1-9

It is strange to us to hear God plotting to confuse his people as though he is fearful of their power. The writers of Genesis do not expect us to take these words as the literal words of God. They expect us to hear the irony. God is not afraid of us. It is we who want to be like him, not the other way round.

So the words put into God's mouth are ours, but the action is God's. Over and over again, God has to act to restrain people because they have forgotten that they are not God and cannot act independently of the limits of the creation. In Genesis 3, they eat forbidden fruit, in Genesis 4, they start to kill, in Genesis 6, they breed with the Nephilim. Each time, God acts to bring human beings and nature back into some kind of proper relation, but each time, people wander off again.

After the Flood, Noah and his sons were told to set off and populate the whole of the world, but now we find this group of people preferring to huddle together, rather than do their duty by the earth. The alienation between people and earth is one of the deep underlying effects of the story that Genesis tells and that we now live in.

COLLECT

God of all mercy,
your Son proclaimed good news to the poor,
release to the captives,
and freedom to the oppressed:
anoint us with your Holy Spirit
and set all your people free
to praise you in Christ our Lord.

Monday 28 January

Psalms 40, **108** *or* 123, 124, 125, **126**
Genesis 11.27 – 12.9
Matthew 26.1-16

Genesis 11.27 – 12.9

It has been a long time since we last heard God speaking to anyone. He spoke to himself in the earlier part of this chapter, but the last human being he spoke to was Noah, and considering how much of Genesis 10 and 11 is genealogies, telling us the generations between Noah and Abram, that is a very long time. It was a long time, too, between Cain and Abel and Noah. The daily conversations of the Garden of Eden are long gone.

But, all the same, the God who now speaks to Abram is not a stranger, even if direct speech with him has been in short supply. Abram knows who he is and how to build altars to him.

Just as with Noah, God breaks his silence now to give Abram a strange command with huge consequences attached. Noah's obedience saved creation, and Abram's is the start of that creation's new relationship with God. So Abram sets off, in search of a land, with no idea how God will deliver, considering that the land already has inhabitants, but setting up altars everywhere he goes, as symbols of his trust.

Spare a thought for the families, dragged along willy-nilly behind their Patriarch. Wives and children don't get to hear God's command, but they, too, have to be obedient.

COLLECT

God our creator,
who in the beginning
commanded the light to shine out of darkness:
we pray that the light of the glorious gospel of Christ
may dispel the darkness of ignorance and unbelief,
shine into the hearts of all your people,
and reveal the knowledge of your glory
    in the face of Jesus Christ your Son our Lord,
who is alive and reigns with you,
in the unity of the Holy Spirit,
one God, now and for ever.

Genesis 13.2-end

Perhaps Abram doesn't really believe the bit about God giving him the land. Perhaps he's just decided to settle for the considerable wealth that his obedience to God seems to have brought him. His travels have increased his livestock and money well beyond what he might have expected if he had stayed at home. Perhaps his imagination cannot quite deal with the concept of 'having' a land. He and his family are nomads, who expect to carry everything with them, and move from one place to another to meet the needs of the herds. What do they want with a single land, anyway? So perhaps Abram is just listening to God politely and carrying on regardless. It does look a little like that, when he quite lightly suggests that Lot should have any part of the territory he likes the look of. Should Abram really be doing that with the land that God has promised?

With hindsight, after the generations of terrible fighting over the land of Israel, it is strange to see how apparently negligent Abram was, here at the beginning of the story. But perhaps his generous unconcern is the right attitude to God's promised land?

God of heaven,
you send the gospel to the ends of the earth
and your messengers to every nation:
send your Holy Spirit to transform us
by the good news of everlasting life
in Jesus Christ our Lord.

COLLECT

Wednesday 30 January

Genesis 14

So far, our focus on Abram has been quite narrow. He did have a bit of a skirmish with Pharaoh in chapter 12 but, on the whole, the other inhabitants of the land through which Abram is driving his flocks have been very much in the background.

But now Abram enters the world stage in a big way. The kings who are fighting it out don't initially take any notice of Abram – he has nothing to do with the struggle they are involved in. It is just Lot's bad luck that he gets caught up in it, because the area that he chose to settle in happened to be in the middle of the fighting.

So it is to protect his family, not to defend the land, that Abram gets involved, but he quickly proves to be a heroic warrior and a cunning strategist. King Melchizedek of Salem pays Abram the compliment of saying that Abram's God must be 'God Most High', the name usually reserved for the most important of the Canaanite gods. Melchizedek must have imagined that his statesman-like gesture would go down in history. He does not realize that he and his kingdom of 'Salem' will actually be remembered because of the descendants of this nomadic fighter, and that he, Melchizedek, will barely count when history remembers Jerusalem's kings.

COLLECT

God our creator,
who in the beginning
commanded the light to shine out of darkness:
we pray that the light of the glorious gospel of Christ
may dispel the darkness of ignorance and unbelief,
shine into the hearts of all your people,
and reveal the knowledge of your glory
    in the face of Jesus Christ your Son our Lord,
who is alive and reigns with you,
in the unity of the Holy Spirit,
one God, now and for ever.

Thursday 31 January

Genesis 15

It sounds, at the start of this chapter, as though Abram is slightly regretting his decision not to take any of the spoils of the battle he won in chapter 14. It's all very well for God to promise Abram protection and reward, but without a son to inherit the promised land, none of it means much, Abram grumbles. Winning that battle seems to have made Abram much more willing to stand up for himself, even in relation to God.

So God enters into a ritual, binding promise that Abram will understand. The cut-up animals represent what will happen to the person who breaks the promise, and the same ritual is described in Jeremiah 34.18. But in this case, God takes the responsibility solely on himself. Whoever breaks the covenant, God will pay. Christian ears can hear this promise reverberating through the centuries.

This is a sombre ritual and the message God gives Abram is similarly dark. He does not just concentrate on the promise of land; he also tells Abram some of the struggle that is to come. Abram will get the son he longs for, and his descendants will get the land, but none of it will be easy. This covenant is appropriately made in blood, smoke and darkness.

God of heaven,
you send the gospel to the ends of the earth
and your messengers to every nation:
send your Holy Spirit to transform us
by the good news of everlasting life
in Jesus Christ our Lord.

COLLECT

Friday 1 February

Genesis 16

Despite the dark solemnity of the ritual by which God has just bound himself to Abram, Abram seems to have forgotten God's promise or, at the very least, to have decided it's best to have a back-up plan.

Strictly speaking, it is Sarai's plan, so perhaps Abram just hadn't communicated his conversations with God to her very clearly. These things do happen in the best-regulated families. But he certainly need not have co-operated with her idea. Was the mighty conqueror of chapter 14 really just a hen-pecked husband?

In her desperate longing for a child, Sarai abandons self-knowledge and decides that she is willing to let her slave-girl be a surrogate for them. This must be what God meant, Sarai decides; God helps those who help themselves. But, of course, it all goes horribly wrong, because Sarai cannot actually live with the reality of the changed relationships she has created.

Naturally, it isn't Sarai who has to pay for the mess made by their lack of faith in God – it is the slave-girl, Hagar. God's provision for her and her child, here and in chapter 21, is one of the most moving aspects of this tangled story. God does not make victims, however hard we try to force him to.

COLLECT

God our creator,
who in the beginning
commanded the light to shine out of darkness:
we pray that the light of the glorious gospel of Christ
may dispel the darkness of ignorance and unbelief,
shine into the hearts of all your people,
and reveal the knowledge of your glory
    in the face of Jesus Christ your Son our Lord,
who is alive and reigns with you,
in the unity of the Holy Spirit,
one God, now and for ever.

Psalms **48**, 146
Exodus 13.1-16
Romans 12.1-5

Saturday 2 February

The Presentation of Christ

Romans 12.1-5

It is hard to imagine exactly how this notion of ourselves as living sacrifices sounded to Paul's readers. For Jewish Christians of this period, before the destruction of the temple in AD 70, there is only one place where sacrifices should be offered, which is by the priests of the Jerusalem temple. Gentile Christians, too, would be familiar with animal sacrifices. So for both groups, Paul is invoking a familiar sacred, ceremonial ritual, but changing it dramatically. Now we are to be the sacrifice; the offering we make is not external, but utterly personal.

Paul is trying to convey the sacredness of the new life in Christ. The blood, smoke and fire of the sacrificial system were all outward signs of the holiness of what was being done. For Christians, the outward signs are changed lives. We are to be united by this sacrifice, not just as worshippers used to be, for those moments while the ritual is being performed, but always. Our separate existence is as completely vanished as the life of the sacrificed animal. We are now a different entity, in Christ.

Almighty and ever-living God,
clothed in majesty,
whose beloved Son was this day presented in the Temple,
in substance of our flesh:
grant that we may be presented to you
with pure and clean hearts,
by your Son Jesus Christ our Lord,
who is alive and reigns with you,
in the unity of the Holy Spirit,
one God, now and for ever.

COLLECT

Book 2
Reflections for Daily Prayer: Lent to Pentecost

Publication date: January 2008

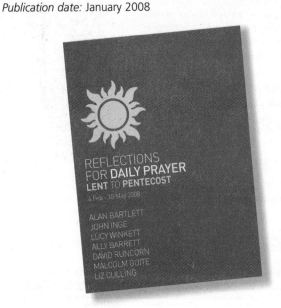

Contributers: Alan Bartlett, John Inge, Lucy Winkett,
Ally Barrett, David Runcorn, Malcolm Guite, Liz Culling

£3.99 978 0 7151 4152 6

Reflections for Daily Prayer is published four times a year
– October, January, April and July – and is available from
all good Christian bookshops. You can also obtain it
direct from the publishers (see page 58).

Common Worship: Daily Prayer

Daily Prayer is ideal for anyone
wanting to follow a regular pattern
of prayer, praise and Bible reading.
The material may be used in small
groups or individually.

£20.00 (Hardback)
978 0 7151 2073 6
202 x 125mm, 896 pages

Time to Pray

Compact, soft-case volume offers a user-friendly
resource for praying through the week.
The simple, accessible structure
allows even those with little time
on their hands the opportunity to
'recharge' for a few minutes
each day. Includes Prayer During
the Day (for every single day of
the week), Night Prayer and
selected psalms from *Common
Worship: Daily Prayer*. To be used
by individuals or small groups.

£12.99 (Soft case)
978 0 7151 2122 7
199 x 125mm, 112 pages

Reflections for Daily Prayer

Subscribe today

For more information on the *Reflections* series, ordering and subscriptions visit **www.dailyprayer.org.uk**

Annual UK subscriptions for four editions	£17.50
Europe	£19.00
Rest of world	£21.50

(all include postage and packing)

It is also possible to arrange gift subscriptions.

Prices correct at time of going to press.